Falling in Love Again

Redirecting Your Earthly Rejection to Eternal Restoration

Dr. Meg Hart

Dedication

This book is dedicated to my Lord and Savior Jesus, the One who rescued me from a life of loneliness disappointment and despair.

I would like to thank my amazing parents Barbara and Harold Hart for their love, support and encouragement.

I would like to thank my beautiful sisters Kate and Marie and their families for always believing in me.

I thank my mommom Stella Tedesco who has loved me and been a true model of Christ's love and acceptance in my life.

I would like to thank my pastor Dr. Jamie Morgan and my Life Church Family for their encouragement, mentorship and friendship.

I also dedicate this book to my beloved and beautiful daughter Mackenzie, who is my miracle, joy and gift from God.

Contents

Foreword

Rejection hurts. Repeated rejection splinters the soul.

As a pastor, I frequently encounter people who struggle with rejection and abandonment issues. They initially seek my counsel because of addictive behavior, feelings of unworthiness, relationship problems, depression, shame, loneliness, or offense – but the root, in many cases, is rejection.

Which of us has gone through life unscathed by rejection? Most have felt its sting. Unfortunately, many Christians are still in desperate need of healing and restoration. If not received, the enemy will continue to use the pain of rejection to prohibit them from enjoying their highest inheritance and cause them to limp through their Christian walk. Don't let that be you!

The splinter of rejection is about to be removed from your soul!

Like a skilled surgeon, Dr. Meg Hart, in her important book, *Falling in Love Again: Redirecting Your Earthly Rejection to Eternal Restoration*, uses Holy Spirit tweezers to remove the splinter of rejection from the depths of your soul so you can experience God's best for your life. Her unique book will position you for God to blast the barrier that has stood between you and the abundant life that Jesus provided on the cross.

With honesty and transparency, Dr. Meg shares her painful story of repeated rejection and the glorious healing she received from her one true love, Jesus Christ. She will help you apply the life-changing Word of God to your life so you can obtain freedom from the pain of rejection and fall in love again…this time for eternity!

I have the honor of being Dr. Meg Hart's pastor. I have known her for twenty-eight years and have seen her walk out each chapter of the story you are about to read.

She is a leader in the body of Christ, a prolific teacher of the Bible, and an anointed preacher; her knowledge and love of Scripture ooze from every page. Meg has pushed through every trial the enemy has sent and has pressed forward to God for the sake of the call.

Her genuine love for people, servant's heart, and passion to see other's set free, compelled her to document her journey for the benefit of others. Dr. Meg is the absolute best one to write this book.

Has your soul been splintered because of the pain of rejection? Finally receive the restoration for which you have yearned. Turn the page and get ready to receive your healing!

Dr. Jamie Morgan
Senior Pastor, Life Church, Williamstown, NJ

Introduction

Are you suffering from a broken heart? Has life brought you great disappointment? Have you felt so lonely for so long that you are ready to finally fall in love? There was a woman named Ruth in the Bible who suffered from a broken heart. When we hear the story of Ruth, we as women sometimes tend to focus on one thing...

"Lord Jesus, give me my Boaz!" We see it plastered all over social media on pretty pictures and hopes and dreams, of whatever that "Boaz" looks like to us. A husband, a provision, someone or something to give us identity and purpose.

There is nothing wrong with wanting a Boaz in your life, but I want to give you a new perspective on the story. The story was not just about Ruth getting her Boaz, it was a love story of God creating a revelation, redirection and restoration in her life through His great love. Through my personal testimony and Biblical examples of people trying to find love or fall in love again, I encourage you to take a journey with me, as we redirect life's pain and rejection to hope and restoration!

Chapter 1

Revelation

Many if you reading this right now are feeling overwhelmed with the feeling that you will never find true love. You see those around you who appear to be happy and fulfilled, but you stopped believing that you will. I am here to tell you not to throw in the towel when it comes to falling in love again. Let's begin the journey together to reveal all God wants to show you for your life and destiny.

When we begin the journey of overcoming rejection, we have an experience with God and must make a conscious decision to leave our old ways of living, thinking and expecting. We decide to shift from our natural desires to the supernatural desires of God.

In the Book of Ruth in the Bible, we learn the backstory of Ruth and her family's heartbreak. Ruth, Naomi, Ruth's mother-in-law, and Orpah Ruth's sister-in-law suffered great loss. When their husbands died and their lives as they knew it were gone forever, they sought to rebuild their identities. Naomi was returning home to Judah and her hometown Bethlehem, where God dwelled and provided among His people.

Naomi gave both of her daughters-in-laws a choice to start their lives over again. They could return to their land, their gods and their familiar ways of life. Naomi herself had an identity crisis. With her husband and sons gone, she did not want Ruth and Orpah to suffer the same fate.

Orpah chose to go back to her familiar life and ties, but Ruth had a revelation. During her years with Naomi, she experienced a connection with Almighty God and was willing to leave everything she knew behind and follow to where He was leading her.

She also had a deep love for Naomi and wanted to be there to care for and support her.

But Ruth said, "Don't force me to leave you; don't make me go home. Where you go, I go; and where you live, I'll live. Your people are my people, your God is my god; where you die, I'll die, and that's where I'll be buried, so help me GOD—not even death itself is going to come between us!"(Ruth 1:16-17)

Once you have an encounter with Almighty God and a revelation of His great love for you, you will be willing to go where He calls you to go and serve who He calls you to serve. Once you encounter His great unfailing love, you will be willing to change your life's direction to His direction, so that He can fulfill His restoration in you, and His great and mighty plans through you for generations to come!

Have you lost hope because of a loss or tragedy in your life? Do you know areas that you need to turn away and be redirected from? Have you established your identity by your family, status, relationships over God?

Naomi was focused on the loss of her husband, sons and self-proclaimed/societal identity. She feared that God had abandoned her and that moving forward she would be rejected.

Even though Naomi was going to need some redirection in her outlook, there was still an awareness that she needed to be where God was. We do not fully understand why they left their home and what may have lured them to Moab. However, it was time to change direction. Maybe some of you are in this state right now. I encourage you to ask God for a fresh outlook and be willing to redirect yourself even through pain and disappointment.

Reflection Time

Once you have an encounter with Almighty God and a revelation of His great love for you, you will be willing to go where He calls you to go and serve who He calls you to serve.

---

1. What does your "Boaz" look like right now?

_____

_____

_____

_____

_____

_____

_____

_____

_____

_____

2. What disappointments are you currently facing?

_____

_____

_____

_____

_____

_____

_____

_____

_____

_____

_____

3. If you are angry with God right now, are you willing to ask for a fresh revelation of truth with whatever you are facing?

_____

_____

_____

_____

_____

_____

_____

_____

_____

_____

_____

_____

Chapter 2

You Are Not Forgotten

Naomi, accompanied by Ruth, finally came back home. People recognized Naomi, but she was not the same. She chose to take an identity of shame, bitterness and depression. Her life did not turn out the way she thought. She left her life in Bethlehem full of hopes and dreams and now returned empty.

She said, "Don't call me Naomi; call me Bitter. The Strong One has dealt me a bitter blow. I left here full of life, and GOD has brought me back with nothing but the clothes on my back. Why would you call me Naomi? God certainly doesn't. The Strong One ruined me." (Ruth 1:20-21)

There are some of you who have held onto bitterness and resentment to God because your earthly lives did not turn out as expected. For those who are single, you may have expected to be married by now. For those divorced, I'm sure you didn't sign up for that to happen. For those who are widowed, you may not have expected to lose your spouse, and cannot imagine a future without them. For those wanting to have children, or a obtain certain job, home, lifestyle, etc., things may have not turned out the way you dreamed they would. For those of you who have children, maybe you have faced great disappointments, or they have walked away from you and God, and your hearts are empty and broken.

It is so easy to believe that God does not care about your life. You have held on to anger or have been lied to by the enemy that God has failed you somehow because life was or is not what you expected.

You are not forgotten.

Amid your joy, pain, successes and failures, you are not forgotten.

In an age of people pleasing, social media and instant gratification, we long for those "likes," "loves" and "wows." Earthly approval and affirmation are nice perks in life, but we cannot spiritually survive on those things. There will be times where people are too busy, distracted, careless or aloof to what is going on in your life. You may feel as though nobody cares. You may feel that people do not get you because all they see is what in on the surface. You may feel forgotten because you are so busy giving and pouring out to others that nobody is even aware of your need to be remembered.

You may feel forgotten, but you are not.

God sees your tears. He understands your pain. He hears your sighs of frustration. He already knew that others would fail to remember or notice you, and He says to you today, "I have not forgotten. I remember you."

- God did not forget Ruth and Naomi when they lost everything.

- God did not forget Noah and his family on the ark when they were obedient to His warning.

- God did not forget Joseph when he was in the pit and prison when he dreamed of rising up to do great exploits for God.

- God did not forget Job when he lost everything.

- God did not forget the widow who gave her last meal.

- God did not forget Abraham and Sarah when they were promised a nation of descendants.

- God did not forget Esther when she was not called by the king for 30 days.

- God did not forget His people as they wandered the wilderness and were taken into captivity.

- God did not forget Hannah, who longed for a child.

- God did not forget David running for his life.

- God did not forget His Son when He hung on the cross to die for us.

- God did not forget followers of Christ who were hidden, imprisoned and persecuted.

God is the same yesterday, today and forever. He remembered then and He remembers now. He never changes! "For the Lord will not forsake His people; neither will He abandon His inheritance" (Ps. 94:14).

God knows, remembers and notices each and every one of you every second of every day. He has already provided a way of escape from your pain and sin, and already had your plan and destiny written out before you were born and for all of eternity. No matter what takes place in this imperfect world or in our imperfect lives, God will never forget you! "Nevertheless, for the sake of Your abundant mercy, You did not completely destroy them or forsake them. Indeed, You are a gracious and merciful God" (Nehemiah 9:31).

The question is not really "Why am I forgotten?" The question should be "What am I forgetting?"

Here are five crucial truths to remember when you feel forgotten:

1. **What does God's Word say about how He remembers His children?** "For the Lord your God is a merciful God, He will not abandon you or destroy you or forget the covenant of your fathers which He swore to them" (Deuteronomy 4:31). Start studying the times God's mercy, forgiveness and love time and time again. Highlight key verses.

2. **Have you remembered to get quiet before God?**

Remember to take time to get quiet before the Holy Spirit and let Him speak to You. Have a journal or recorder ready so you can go back and be encouraged when you feel forgotten. "Those who know Your name will put their trust in You, for You, Lord, have not forsaken those who seek You" (Psalm 9:10).

3. **Have you remembered the most important things God chooses not to?**

When you confess your sins, he remembers them no more. "I will forgive their iniquity, and I will remember their sin no more" (Jer. 31:34c). I, even I, am He who blots out your transgressions for My own sake and will not remember your sins" (Isaiah 43:25).

When you accept Jesus as your Lord and Savior, your past sins are forgotten. His mercy, grace and restoration are yours for the asking. When Jesus took His last breath, He remembered you. When He rose to life and now sits at the right hand of Father God, He remembers you. He sent us His Holy Spirit to help us remember.

4. **Do you remember that Satan hates you and everyone else on this earth, and wants to deceive you into believing that God has forsaken you?**

Are you taking your authority in Jesus and standing against the lies of the enemy? If you truly believe God has forgotten and forsaken you, you are being deceived, and it's time to stand up and remind the enemy that he is already defeated! "Be sober and watchful, because your adversary the devil walks around as a roaring lion, seeking whom he may devour. Resist him firmly in the faith, knowing that the same afflictions are experienced by your brotherhood throughout the world" (1 Peter 5:8-9).

4. **Who can you remember?**
When you feel forgotten, step out and see who else may feel the same.

Just like Ruth would not leave Naomi, and decided to care for her, maybe there is a single parent who could use a phone call or a bag of groceries. Maybe there is a senior at a nursing home who could use a smile and a visit. Maybe there is a child having a rough time at home who could use a night of bowling or some ice cream. Maybe there is a pastor who could use a note of encouragement, a cup of coffee or some extra prayer. "If you give yourself to the hungry and satisfy the afflicted soul, then your light shall rise in obscurity, and your darkness shall become as the noonday" (Isaiah 58:10).

During these seasons of feeling forgotten, be deliberate to remember God's promises for His children now and forevermore. He is with you and has not forgotten!

Reflection Time

God sees your tears. He understands your pain. He hears your sighs of frustration. He already knew that others would fail to remember or notice you, and He says to you today, "I have not forgotten. I remember you."

1. What areas in your life do you feel
    forgotten?

    _____

    _____

    _____

    _____

    _____

    _____

    _____

    _____

    _____

2. What examples that you just read gave you
    encouragement regarding God's care for
    you?

    _____

    _____

    _____

    _____

    _____

    _____

    _____

    _____

_____

_____

3. Who can you reach out to who may feel
   forgotten?

_____

_____

_____

_____

_____

_____

_____

_____

_____

_____

Chapter 3

Redirection

Before we focus on getting back to our "Boaz" let's look at how Ruth redirected her circumstances

As stated earlier, Ruth was willing to redirect her life and go where she was drawn to God and where He wanted her to be. She was willing to serve others despite her pain. If she wanted to be comfortable, she would have gone back to her old life and where she would find identity familiarity. However, the love of God that she experienced through Naomi, and perhaps even her father-in-law and husband, showed her something different than any earthly relationship.

God was drawing her into her purpose through His love. It did not look appealing in the natural, and certainly was not the way any of them thought life would take them, but God was going to use it all for His glory if they were willing to be redirected to His ways and plans.

Friends, I am here to tell you today that God loves you. Our earthly expectations do not always turn out the way we want because we live in a broken, sinned-filled world. People fail. We fail. If we leave the place where God can speak to us and show us His plans, we create our own plans of how our lives on the earth are supposed to be, leaving us bitterly disappointed when things do not turn out as we planned it.

All of the things I mentioned earlier are wonderful things, and there is nothing wrong with desiring those things! However, now, more than ever, we need to make the first thing the first thing!

When is the last time you really got quiet before God and asked for His perspective on your current situation or your future? For you single ladies, maybe God has a mighty call on your life that for this season does not include a spouse. Maybe God has a great call on your life, but you are too busy to be mad at Him because of loss or disappointments in your life. Some of you have been chasing the dream of seeking an identity through a relationship with someone else, and you are running in circles going nowhere.

Maybe you have kids and have made them your world and are waiting for them to grow up; maybe you have rooted your identity and purpose in them. There is nothing wrong with loving and serving those around us, but are you first building and growing your relationship with Jesus? Are you giving Him your time, worship and commitment before anything or anyone else? If we are all honest, we can all say we need to redirect certain areas of our lives! It is so easy to allow our earthly roles take precedent over our spiritual identities and God-given specific purposes to further His Kingdom.

Life does not begin based on earthy relationships.

You may be waiting to really live after you find that best friend, spouse, have your own children, or be part of a supportive work team or a gain a platform of ministry partners. You wait to enjoy life until you have these things, then wallow in disappointment, self-pity and depression when you don't get what you longed for. Until one day, you wake up and realize this precious time on earth is flying by.

God wants you to start living!

Before anyone in this world had a chance to accept or reject you, God already designed, accepted and loved you before you even took your first breath on this earth! How amazing is that?

Everything in your life was designed to fulfill the call on your life, and God provided the way to enjoy and love life through Jesus.

"[God], making known to us the mystery of His will, according to His good pleasure, which He purposed in Himself, as a plan for the fullness of time, to unite all things in Christ, which are in heaven and on earth. In Him also we have received an inheritance, being predestined according to the purpose of Him who works all things according to the counsel of His own will, that we, who were the first to hope in Christ, should live for the praise of His glory" (Ephesians 1:9-12).

Just like Ruth had to be patient and wait, here are some practical ways you can start enjoying life while you wait on God's plan and timing:

1. **If you are longing for a friend, start living.** Draw close to Jesus, the friend who sticks closer than a brother (Prov. 18:24). Pray for God's hand-selected friendships and ask Him to show you who you can befriend. Go volunteer at a nursing home, hospital or foster care outreach. Go find someone sitting alone at the lunch table. The possibilities are endless.

2. **If you are waiting for a spouse, start living.**
Draw close to Jesus, the lover of your soul. Pour you love, devotion and faithfulness to the one who unconditionally and radically loves you. Place your heart's desires for a spouse into God's hands and enjoy your life. God would not have miss out on your heavenly assignment, whether you are single or married. If it's flowers, candy, jewelry and vacations you want, then make them happen. Treat yourself. Take a mission trip. Experience this beautiful world God gave us.

3. **If you are waiting to become a parent, start living.**

Do not be limited by your circumstances. Change your perspective. Pour your love out to the babies and children in your extended family, church or a community. Foster or adopt children. Sponsor a child overseas. God can bless you with opportunities to parent children in a multitude of ways.

4. **While you wait to connect and fit in with co-workers, start living.**
Ask God to help you be a shining light for Him. He may or may not have you build earthly

relationships with them but will use you in that season to be a light and living testimony. Listen, observe, pray for them and be ready to do whatever God leads you to do. When you go about His business, He will take care of yours.

5. **If you are waiting for a platform of supporters, start living**.

God's platform for you may be different than what you think. Be faithful with whatever He gives you. Start sharing your testimony with one person. Volunteer and serve at your local church wherever the need is communicated. Ask God in faith for a platform to reach the world, but let revival start in your own heart and life. Do not despise small beginnings (Zech. 4:10). If you are faithful with the little, you will be ready to be faithful for the larger things God has for you (Luke 16:10).

The purpose for your life was predestined before you were ever born. The decision to enjoy your life and walk out your call from God is up to you. Proverbs 16:9 reminds us, "A man's heart devises his way, but the Lord directs his steps."

The God who created you is with you always and will give you everything you need to enjoy life.

Remember, your life does not begin based on your earthly relationships. Start living!

God had a plan for you to share the Good News of Jesus with a lost and dying world before you were even born! Again, the roles we have on this earth as an earthly daughter, sister, wife, mother, employee and friend are all important, but again, if you make the first thing the first thing, you can serve best in these roles because you are living your identity as a daughter of the most high God and as a co-heir with your Lord Jesus Christ! You can and will have total satisfaction in your life because you are walking and serving according to His plan!

Ruth was willing to leave her old life, follow the new life and serve God and others. She did not leave the old life to get her a "Boaz," but she left and served because she had an encounter with the love of God.

In Ruth 2: 1-9, Ruth decided to do all she could to help her mother-in-law. She decided to glean from the fields for provision. She was going to need to trust daily that God would provide what was needed. She had to get out of bed, go to the field, expect in faith that there would work for her to do and food to gather for her and her mother-in-law.

One day Ruth, the Moabite foreigner, said to Naomi, "I'm going to work; I'm going out to glean among the sheaves, following after some harvester who will treat me kindly." (Ruth 2:2)

There are times in the redirection in our lives that we need to step out in faith and work hard at what God has called us to do: serve others, trust that He will supply every need and give us the strength to do what He has called us to do. Ruth worked diligently and kept her focus on what was called to do. She was not seeking a "Boaz" but God's plan to serve others.

Redirection is not always glamorous and not always easy. It takes humility, faith, trust and perseverance. However, when we make God our first love and trust that He will provide and meet our needs, He encounters us with His direction, provision and favor. God rewards us well for what we do for Him.

As we are redirected, people start to notice. When Boaz heard about Ruth's story and her faithfulness to Naomi and desire to seek help from God, He extended favor to her. He allowed her to glean from his field, drink from his well and eat from his bread.

Then Boaz spoke to Ruth: "Listen, my daughter. From now on don't go to any other field to glean—stay right here in this one. And stay close to my young women. Watch where they are harvesting and follow them. And don't worry about a thing; I've given orders to my servants not to harass you. When you get thirsty, feel free to go and drink from the water buckets that the servants have filled." (Ruth 2:8-9)

As we make Jesus our first love, He will extend his favor toward us and we will lack nothing. He is our Provider. He is our Living Water. He is our Bread of Life!

When Ruth came home with her bag of blessings and report of the kindness of Boaz, Naomi's eyes were opened to the truth! She stopped feeling sorry for herself and what she lost and saw that God was still there.

Naomi said to her daughter-in-law, "Why, God bless that man! God hasn't quite walked out on us after all! He still loves us, in bad times as well as good!" Naomi went on, "That man, Ruth, is one of our circle of covenant redeemers, a close relative of ours!" (Ruth 2:20)

Friends, God hasn't walked out on you after all! He still loves you, in the good times and the bad.

Ruth gleaned from the fields until the harvest was over. She did not meet Boaz and then live happily ever after. She served God, was a testimony to Boaz, his workers and Naomi, and worked at the task at hand until it was finished.

Are you willing to serve God in whatever He called you to? She placed her identity and trust in Him first and THEN was able to serve in her earthly role and serve Him and others! Seek Him First and all these things will be added!

"What I'm trying to do here is to get you to relax, to not be so preoccupied with getting, so you can respond to God's giving. People who don't know God and the way he works fuss over these things, but you know both God and how he works. Steep your life in God-reality, God-initiative, God-provisions. Don't worry about missing out. You'll find all your everyday human concerns will be met." (Matthew 6:32-33)

As I said before, your earthly roles are vital, but you must seek and make the first thing the first thing.

Reflection Time

Friends, God hasn't walked out on you after all! He still loves you, in the good times and the bad.

---

1. Are you willing to serve God with whatever He calls you to? What struggles do you have accomplishing this?

_____

_____

_____

_____

_____

_____

_____

_____

_____

_____

2. Are you willing to love and serve God and others before yourself? What barriers are stopping you?

_____

_____

_____

_____

_____

_____

_____

_____

_____

3. Read Ruth Chapter 2. What ways can you start overcoming challenges of serving God and others through her example?

_____

_____

_____

_____

_____

_____

_____

_____

_____

_____

Chapter 4
Restoration

Naomi sensed that it was time for Ruth's restoration. Again, Boaz did not come to her riding on a horse with a dozen roses and some cheesy lines and whisk her away to bliss! This was about a willingness to wait for God's perfect timing and be content with whatever path God chose for her. She was 100% obedient and willing to humble herself to God for each step.

First, Ruth did not force herself on Boaz. She again with humility, courage and integrity, waited for Him to respond.

Are you patiently waiting for the restoration to come? Are you following God's word regarding each step and walking in integrity to wait for it? Or will you compromise, and go take what you want for yourself? Many times, our plans fail because we skip a step or create our own way to manipulate to get what we want! Restoration comes when we wait on the Lord with the right heart, attitude and intentions! She was also willing to pursue God's best, not necessarily what her earthly mind would count as the best choice? No matter what your seeking, ask is it is a good idea or a God idea!

Boaz represented redemption. He was a close kinsman redeemer to Naomi, and if was he willing to redeem, he could bring restoration back to the family. Because Ruth acted according to God's plan, timing and steps, she found someone who was willing to love and care for her! However, now Boaz had to abide by God's steps and timing.

He said, "God bless you, my dear daughter! What a splendid expression of love! And when you could have had your pick of any of the young men around. And now, my dear daughter, don't you worry about a thing; I'll do all you could want or ask. Everybody in town knows what a courageous woman you are—a real prize! You're right, I am a close relative to you, but there is one even closer than I am. So stay the rest of the night. In the morning, if he wants to exercise his customary rights and responsibilities as the closest covenant redeemer, he'll have his chance; but if he isn't interested, as GOD lives, I'll do it. Now go back to sleep until morning." (Ruth 3:10-13)

There was someone closer as kinsman redeemer who could claim her as his wife. However, God worked everything out for Ruth, Naomi and even Boaz himself to have His best!

When you give yourselves to your first love Jesus, without anything in the way, even if it is a good thing, He will not take away your dreams and identities! Now that your heart is aligned with the One who is perfect love, you can now experience and share His perfect love with others. Your life will have a renewed purpose and others will be eternally impacted!

What started out as a revelation of the Power of God, redirection to leave the past pain, present disappointments and fears of the future behind, and serve and obey God with an open, humble and obedient heart, gave Ruth and the lives she impacted restoration beyond measure or expectation. Her Boaz came in the natural, but true love encountered her way before he ever crossed her path. She fell in love with God first, and her restoration came as being part of the bloodline of the greatest redeemer of all, the Lord Jesus Christ! Her life and testimony helped change the heart of Naomi, who was ready to give up.

The townswomen said to Naomi, "Blessed be GOD! He didn't leave you without family to carry on your life. May this baby grow up to be famous in Israel! He'll make you young again! He'll take care of you in old age. And this daughter-in-law who has brought him into the world and loves you so much, why, she's worth more to you than seven sons!" (Ruth 4:14-15)

Ruth's journey from loss to restoration is a testimony of hope for those who want to fall in love again!

If you are feeling empty, here are three ways to let the love of Jesus fill you, so you can pour out to others.

1. **Fill the voids in your heart with the love of Jesus.**
Nobody on this earth will ever love you more. We may feel the pain of earthly loss, but through faith we can connect our hearts to the One who can bring us eternal healing and fulfillment.

That Christ may dwell in your hearts through faith; that you, being rooted and grounded in love, may be able to comprehend with all saints what is the breadth and length and depth and height, and to know the love of Christ which surpasses knowledge; that you may be filled with all the fullness of God (Eph. 3:17-19).

2. **Live each moment eternally focused, fulfilling the Great Commission from the one who loved us the most.**

Jesus died so that we could reconnected to the love of God for all of eternity. The pain we feel now is only temporary. By faith, choose to accept and show His love.

"I have been crucified with Christ and I no longer live, but Christ lives in me. The life I now live in the body, I live by faith in the Son of God, who loved me and gave himself for me" (Gal. 2:20).

Just like Ruth did for Naomi, reach out to others who need love, compassion and kindness. If you are sad you didn't receive gifts or flowers, go buy them for someone else. If you have not been told that you were loved or valued, go find others who feel the same and tell them you love and care for them. Serve others with the humility and kindness of Christ, and your heart will be so full you can hardly contain it!

If there is any encouragement in Christ, if any comfort of love, if any fellowship of the Spirit, if any compassion and mercy, then fulfill my joy and be like-minded, having the same love, being in unity with one mind. Let nothing be done out of strife or conceit, but in humility let each esteem the other better than himself (Phil. 2:1-3).

Never forget that Jesus loves you fully, completely and eternally. Accept, embrace and value that love and introduce Him to as many people as you can!

May our lives and love for God and others be the beacon of light to bring God's revelation, restoration and redirection to others in need!

Reflection Time

Many times, our plans fail because we skip a step or create our own way to manipulate to get what we want! Restoration comes when we wait on the Lord with the right heart, attitude and intentions!

---

1. Do you try and do things in your own strength and timing? What was the result?

_____

_____

_____

_____

_____

_____

_____

_____

_____

_____

2. How can you use Ruth's example to trust God and His timing?

_____

_____

_____

_____

_____

_____

_____

_____

_____

_____

3. Read Ruth 3-4. What inspired you about Ruth and Naomi's triumph despite their great loss?

_____

_____

_____

_____

_____

_____

_____

_____

_____

_____

_____

Chapter 5

My Testimony

I want to share my testimony with you of my revelation, redirection and restoration through a story in which you may have heard somewhere before...

I decided early in life that I was going to get married, have two kids and be famous! I was going to live in a nice house, drive a nice car and help others in need. My life was going to be so happy! I already asked Jesus for this, so I knew I'm going to get what I wanted! I wanted to be like Cinderella and find my prince! I want him to be just like my daddy. I wanted to go with him all over the world and tell others about Jesus!

By the time I was in high school, I realized that life was not what I thought it would be. I thought I would meet my high school sweetheart and live happily ever after. I thought that I would find true love just like in the movies, in the stories I read and what I saw on TV. I kept asking God to conform to my will regarding boys I thought were "the one" to actually be "the one." I didn't know why God wouldn't answer my prayers. I bounced from one boy telling me he loves me, to being rejected again and again. I must not be good enough. I felt very dirty and guilty because I thought an older boy really liked and cared about me. He told me to sneak out and meet him.

Could this be my first real boyfriend? He kissed me in a way I never experienced but things got out of hand. I wanted him to stop but he wouldn't. I was saved that day from being fully violated but when I saw him the next day, he never spoke to me again and denied everything. I felt so embarrassed and ashamed and was violated in more ways than I thought. I was not good enough. I had to prove myself for the next four years of high school with hard work, recognition and gain approval from others so I could feel good again. Sure, I loved God, but I felt like if I was really worthy in His eyes I would not be going through this pain. No boyfriends ever lasted, yet I could never be without one. I was hurt and I hurt others. I felt I was just not worth anything good in the area of relationships, and I would just have to do the best I could and be the best I could be, and maybe there will still be a chance for someone to love and accept me. It was a vicious cycle that lasted for years.

I finally finished high school. I did well for myself. I won several awards and accolades, was a pageant queen and excelled at everything…well except relationships of course! At first, they started out well. Guys said they felt connected to me because of my compassion, kindness and drive. Don't get me wrong; I loved Jesus, learned His Word and wanted to follow Him fully. However, I was convinced that something was wrong with me, or someone here would love me. Things would go great for a while but then it never worked out. I was torn between two worlds, the one I knew God wanted me to live in and serve Him fully, and the one I created in my own imagination and desires. I thought I could have it both ways. I was very wrong.

I graduated and met a whole new group of people who didn't know who I was or where I came from. They brought me into their world, and I thought I finally met the one! We had our walks on the beach hand in hand romantic dinners and the admiration on one another's eyes. Little did I know that he was living in a different world as well.

With a lot of smooth talking and introduction to worldly pleasures I never even thought about pursuing before, I started my path of destruction through the sip of a wine cooler. I had told my new love that I was saving myself for marriage and that it was important to me. However, one night after drinking a homemade concoction at a party, I blacked out. When I woke up, I was no longer a virgin. I had been violated multiple times and cannot recall a single moment. As I went into the shower to try and make myself look and feel clean again, all I could do is cry. Why did this happen? I thought he wanted to wait for me, only finding out later I was just part of a sick game.

I tried to make it right. I was ready to run back to God as a filthy and dirty rag. I told my youth pastor what happened and that I was sorry and wanted to be forgiven. I was later put in front of multiple people who only had the look of disappointment because everyone had such high expectations of me and now it was over. I walked away and never looked back. I hid my shame with a mask of deception. A mask that said that everything was okay.

The remainder of my college years were ones of secret pain. On the outside I was a star student, pageant queen, and the life of every party. From a distance, up on the pedestal, I looked pretty good to those back home and those around me. I went from one destructible relationship to another because I just wanted someone to love me. I was passed around from one abuser to the next. I covered the pain with alcohol, many times behind closed doors where nobody could see the ugly, rejected and worthless image I saw in the mirror.

By the time I married for the first time, I was so good at living a double life that I had everyone convinced that I was okay. I just wanted to love someone and have them love me back. I knew that my childhood dreams were not reality, and because I was dirty and worthless, I could only hope that someone would come along and not see it. I would pray and serve God at church and then go home to countless experiences of mental, physical and emotional abuse. I thought having a baby would bring peace. In my mind, I thought that maybe I wasn't valued as a wife, but I would be as a mother. Maybe it would fix or change things. Sadly, it didn't. People asked, "Why didn't you tell anyone?" I was afraid. I felt like I deserved it because these were the decisions I made, and I was soiled and unworthy to have God's best. Inevitably, the marriage ended in divorce and I was now alone as a single mom.

I still loved God, but I thought I could never be who He intended me to be. I went into hiding and did my best to smile and settle through life. I tried dating but it never worked out.

During that season I had an encounter with God through a woman named Jamie Morgan who is now the senior pastor of my church, Life Church. She told me that God still loved me, I still had a call on my life, and it was time to get up and get moving! Through the years of numbness, I started to feel again. I began going to young adult meetings and church and rededicated my life to Jesus and started to pursue my call to preach the Gospel. I was studying to become a pastor.

Things seemed to be going in the right direction but there was still a missing piece. I declared my love for Jesus, but I did not fully receive His love and healing from my past pain. I still held onto the belief that Jesus loved me, but there would be conditions because of what happened to me and because of the bad choices I made.

I could bring encouragement to so many people but could not fully practice what I preached. This was because I still had not fully returned to my first love. My friends…being in relationship with anyone, especially Jesus, has two be both-sided for it to work! There were still pieces missing and the holes were open enough for me to be deceived once again. Years after my divorce, I met the one I thought was Boaz. I ignored red flags and just saw a worship leader who experienced life pain as well; I thought we could be "broken" together. There is NO such thing!

Two broken things do not make a whole!

His charismatic, humorous and fun demeanor were so different than any relationship I ever had before, so I thought that this had to be it! However, when red flags are present, compromise is committed and the voice of self-fulfillment drowned out the still, small voice saying, "This is not My plan," that relationship also ended with abandonment, insurmountable debt, and a broken family experiencing rejection again. I lost my home, my health was failing, and my heart was once again broken.

Who was I?

I was a modern-day woman at the well.

God pointed me to read John 4. In this book and chapter of the Bible, Jesus revealed truth to the woman at the well, who also suffered from a broken heart, broken promises and broken dreams of love.

Jesus revealed to her that He was the living water, her Savior and her first love.

Jesus replied, "If you only knew who I am and the gift that God wants to give you — you'd ask me for a drink, and I would give to you living water…From here on, worshiping the Father will not be a matter of the right place but with the right heart. For God is a Spirit, and he longs to have sincere worshipers who worship and adore him in the realm of the Spirit and in truth…"You don't have to wait any longer, the Anointed One is here speaking with you — I am the One you're looking for." (John 4:10, 22-23, 26)

As I read this book, it was like He was speaking to me! He was, and He is speaking to you too! He spoke to me with love, and grace, even when the others from the outside looking in saw a twice-divorced throwaway with nothing left to give God in this life. Just like the woman at the well, I experienced a revelation of His love, and a redirection of hope, confidence and life in Him. Like her, I accepted it as truth, walked out in faith and freedom to share my story with you so you can be free!

The woman at the well was able to share Jesus with others because she had a revelation of who He was, redirected her past of pain to a future of hope and was part of God's restoration for others.

All at once, the woman dropped her water jar and ran off to her village and told everyone, "Come and meet a man at the well who told me everything I've ever done! He could be the Anointed One we've been waiting for." Hearing this, the people came streaming out of the village to go see Jesus… So there were many from the Samaritan village who became believers in Jesus because of the woman's testimony: "He told me everything I ever did!" (John 4:28-30)

Like her, I had a decision to make. Last time I ran and hid from God and the call upon my life. Last time I ran into the wrong person's embrace. This time I was at the end of my hopes and dreams but willing to let Jesus in to fully to heal me and show me His plans and dreams. I was no longer in self-denial but revelation that someone radically loved me, and that it was way past due, but not too late…to accept His love fully and completely.

I met Him at the well. He already knew my past sin and shame. He knew I was rejected by so many, even myself.

I dropped everything I thought my life was before, along with my self-imposed will and surrendered my hopes and dreams to Jesus. I started a new journey of freedom and hope with Him, and my life has never been the same.

Reflection Time

I dropped everything I thought my life was before, along with my self-imposed will and surrendered my hopes and dreams to Jesus. I started a new journey of freedom and hope with Him, and my life has never been the same.

1. What part of my testimony can you relate to?

_____
_____
_____
_____
_____
_____
_____
_____
_____
_____
_____

2. What part of the woman at the well's story resonated with you?

_____
_____
_____
_____
_____
_____
_____
_____
_____

3. What specific areas of your past, present or future are you ready to surrender?

_____

_____

_____

_____

_____

_____

_____

_____

_____

_____

_____

Chapter 6

Finding Purpose in the Loneliness

Throughout the Christian walk, people often experience great earthly loneliness. The enemy uses rejection, unrealistic expectations and abandonment from others to convince God's children that they have been forgotten and that God caused the pain to somehow punish them. As believers, we are living in the last days and in critical times. Satan is deceiving Christians to doubt God during times of suffering.

During the great falling-away of the church, people are turning away from God and trying to fill their loneliness with the temporary pleasures of this world. Christians young and old try to find love and acceptance through pornography, partnering in unequally yoked relationships and filling their voids with addiction and self-harm. Some have left the church because they suffered unexpected losses of relationships or deaths of loved ones and have blamed God. Some have isolated themselves from God and others and have taken roots of bitterness, hatred and revenge out on others who have hurt or abused them. Some have become angry with God because they did not yet receive their healing, get married, get the job they wanted or have children the way they thought they would.

After suffering the pain of being raped, going through two painful divorces, losing my home, suffering financially as a single mom and experiencing great pain, rejection in friendships, ministry and working relationships, I understand earthly loneliness.

Like Naomi, I often thought my solitude was a punishment from God. There were times I questioned the purpose for the pain. If I loved others with the love of Christ, why did they reject and abuse me? If I was faithful in my relationships, why were they unfaithful back? If I tithed and gave to God, why did I struggle to make ends meet? If I was loyal at work, why was I isolated and falsely accused? At the end of all of the questions and the tears, I had decisions to make: Was I going to believe in the goodness of God? Was God's Word true? Did Jesus exchange my earthly loneliness and pain at the cross for eternal joy and peace?

After isolating myself, trying things in my own strength, experiencing rejection and loneliness from others and buying into the lies of the enemy, I needed to wake, up, repent, take my stand and trust that I was connected to God no matter how lonely I felt. Because Jesus took my pain on the cross, my temporary earthly pain would be exchanged for eternal joy. "For I consider that the sufferings of this present time are not worthy to be compared with the glory which shall be revealed to us" (Rom. 8:18). God has turned my life around and is continuing to redeem all the pain I experienced. From those seasons of pain, my ministry and calling were birthed to those around the world needing hope of His restoration.

The very gifts of freedom, peace and joy that Jesus died to give are willfully being exchanged for doubt, fear and resentment. It's time to wake up to the enemy's scheme!

Here are four ways to transform that earthly pain and loneliness into kingdom purpose:

1. Remember that Jesus understands all of our pain and suffering.

He experienced every pain we have and will face. "He was despised and rejected of men, a man of sorrows and acquainted with grief. And we hid, as it were, our faces from him; he was despised, and we did not esteem him" (Isa. 53:3). If we think we are alone in our pain and loneliness, we are reminded that Jesus experienced great earthly loneliness and rejection from his family, His followers and those for whom He suffered and died then and now.

2. It's time to stand up and get rude with the devil.

Jesus gave us the gift of salvation. We need to stop exchanging our gift with a thief! Satan is the one who robs us and brings destruction. It's time to stop fighting God and others and put the enemy in his place, which is under our feet: "Finally, my brothers, be strong in the Lord and in the power of His might. Put on the whole armor of God that you may be able to stand against the schemes of the devil. For our fight is not against flesh and blood, but against principalities, against powers, against the rulers of the darkness of this world, and against spiritual forces of evil in the heavenly places. Therefore, take up the whole armor of God that you may be able to resist in the evil day, and having done all, to stand" (Eph. 6:10-13).

3. Thank God for replacing the pain with His purpose.

As we remember God's goodness, trust that He is doing a great work inside of each of us during these lonely times. God did not cause your pain, but He will use it. He can use it to strengthen our faith, build character, protect us from world influences and refine us when sin is exposed. He brings healing to our hearts when we connect with Him, and sometimes everything else falls apart or withers away until we are face-to-face with our heavenly Father who is the only one who can fill the void. The pain we feel now will be turned around for His good. We were never promised a life without pain but that God will walk us through it. He will take that pain, help us overcome and then use it as a testimony to others who are experiencing the same suffering and loneliness. "Blessed be God, the Father of our Lord Jesus Christ, the Father of mercies, and the God of all comfort, who comforts us in all our tribulation, that we may be able to comfort those who are in any trouble by the comfort with which we ourselves are comforted by God" (2 Cor. 1:3-4).

4. Remember that the pain and loss we experience in this life is temporary.

Those in Christ who stand with Him and His Word until the end are promised that one day all pain and loneliness will be gone, and limitless joy, peace and belonging abounds for eternity! But after you have suffered a little while, the God of all grace, who has called us to His eternal glory through Christ Jesus, will restore, support, strengthen, and establish you" (1 Peter 5:10)

Our earthly pain and solitude are only for a season. Take heart, take a stand and connect to the One who will bring you victory, restoration and hope. Jesus understands our pain, but he died and rose again to exchange it for our beautiful testimonies and eternities of everlasting joy and acceptance!

I have been a single mom for over 8 years now. There are moments of earthly loneliness. However, through the eyes of eternity, I have never been more in love than I am right now! God has and is continuing to restore my life. I eventually became an ordained pastor and now endeavor to spend the rest of my life pointing others to Jesus and help others to see their worth and value through God's eyes and decide to fall in love with Jesus now and forever!

In 2015, I founded Restored Women to help others like me fall in love with Jesus all over again, and allow him to reveal His plan, redirect us from everything that is not His best for us and bring the restoration of His love into every area of our lives, so that we may be healed and help bring hope and encouragement to others to fall in love with Him for the first time, or all over again.

My story did not end in rejection, and the woman at the well's story did not end there either. She left her water pot because she found the real source of living water! She told her story to others, pointing them to Jesus, without shame or inhibition.

Many Samaritans from that village committed themselves to Him because of the woman's witness: "He knew all about the things I did. He knows me inside and out!" They asked him to stay on, so Jesus stayed two days. A lot more people entrusted their lives to him when they heard what he had to say. They said to the woman, "We're no longer taking this on your say-so. We've heard it for ourselves and know it for sure. He's the Savior of the world!" (John 39-42)

Today, my ministry as grown to Restored Global, where my vision has expanded to helping those around the world experience the restoration of Jesus and reach their fullest potentials for the Kingdom of God. My story is far from over!

The best part is that your story does not have to end here either! Are you ready for a change in your perspective and future?

Reflection Time

*We were never promised
a life without pain, but
that God will walk us
through it. He will take
that pain, help us
overcome and then use it
as a testimony to others
who are experiencing the
same suffering and
loneliness.*

1. Read John 4. What did you discover for
   your own life?

   _____

   _____

   _____

   _____

   _____

   _____

   _____

   _____

   _____

   _____

   _____

2. Replace three old thoughts with new
   thoughts about your identity through the
   eyes of Jesus!

   _____

   _____

   _____

   _____

   _____

   _____

   _____

   _____

3. Jesus knows all about you, yet He loves and accepts you! What does this free you from?

_____

_____

_____

_____

_____

_____

_____

_____

_____

_____

_____

Chapter 7

It's Your Turn to Redirect Your Rejection into Restoration!

Do you feel devalued by the world? Do you feel that God loves you less because of your past mistakes and hurts? Have you bought into the lies of the enemy and through others who have rejected you and told you that you are unworthy? If you have said yes to even one of these things, then it's time to back to the basics. The words "devalued" and "unworthy" in the same sentence describing a "Christian" is an oxymoron!

If you have allowed the enemy into your mind, emotions and soul with any doubt of your worth, here are six questions to ask yourself.

1. Does God have attributes of unworthiness?
When God created you, He created you in His image. Then God said, "Let us make mankind in our image, after our likeness" (Genesis 1:26). We were created in the image of God, in the likeness of His Son Jesus, and the regenerated Holy Spirit of God lives inside us.

The enemy hates that we were designed in God's image, so since the beginning of time, He has questioned your worth to God and others.

However, God has promised that His love for His children is everlasting. "Indeed, I have loved you with an everlasting love; therefore with lovingkindness I have drawn you" (Jeremiah 31:3).

This is a gift we cannot take for granted. Your Father God, who created and designed you for such a time as this, has given and will always look at you with value and worth.

"Every good gift and every perfect gift is from above and comes down from the Father of lights, with whom is no change or shadow of turning" (James 1:17).

2. Doesn't God choose to greatly use those who the world rejected?

Every major character in God's Word was rejected by others. David wasn't even recognized by his own family as worthy enough to be king. Joseph was rejected in the pit and neglected in the prison. The women at the well, who was rejected by everyone, became a powerful evangelist for Jesus. Many of the disciples were uneducated and unqualified by the world's standards. What made the difference? They were able to do great things for God because they understood that they are the clay and God is the potter. Today, we are called to do great things for God no matter how rejected we are by others. He took us and designed us into valuable and worthy vessels to be poured into and poured out to others.

"But we have this treasure in earthen vessels, the excellency of the power being from God and not from ourselves" (2 Corinthians 4:7).

3. If Jesus died for everyone in this entire world, wasn't that enough to prove your worth?

Your loving Savior came in human form, humbled Himself and was rejected and despised by those He came to save. If Jesus relied on His human emotions or what others thought of Him, He would not have been able to endure the cross. Rather, He knew who He was and what we were to Him, His precious children who were like lambs going to the slaughter. He became that Lamb willingly so that we could live eternally with Him. He thought you were valuable enough when He hung on the cross.

"He was oppressed and afflicted, yet he opened not his mouth; he was brought as a lamb to the slaughter, and as a sheep before its shearers is silent, so he opened not his mouth" (Isaiah 53:7).

God chose you before you ever stepped into this world, and Jesus chose you when He died and rose again because you were and are worth it.

"Just as He chose us in Christ before the foundation of the world, to be holy and blameless before him in love" (Ephesians 1:4).

If you are holy and blameless before God, then you have immeasurable value: "But God, being rich in mercy, because of His great love with which He loved us, even when we were dead in sins, made us alive together with Christ ... that in the coming ages He might show the surpassing riches of His grace in kindness toward us in Christ Jesus" (Eph. 2:4-7).

4. Why do you put stock in what the world thinks when Jesus came to save us from it?

Jesus warned us that the world would hate us.

"If the world hates you, you know that it hated Me before it hated you. If you were of the world, the world would love you as its own. But because you are not of the world, since I chose you out of the world, the world therefore hates you" (John 15:18-19).

Those who did the greatest things for Christ no longer looked to the world for approval, acceptance or self-worth. They saw eternal value that Satan and the world could never take away, tarnish or diminish. They realized that they were in but not of this world.
If we base our worth on what others think of us, then we need to repent and fix our eyes on the one who always calls us worthy, because time is running out.

"See then that you walk carefully, not as fools, but as wise men, making the most of the time because the days are evil" (Ephesians 5:15-16).

5. How can you win the lost for Christ if you do not feel valued or worthy?

This world is not our home.

"But our citizenship is in heaven, from where also we wait for our Savior, the Lord Jesus Christ" (Philippians 3:20).

As citizens of heaven, we should not be sulking or worrying about what others think. As citizens of heaven, we should emulate the beauty, value and worth that God placed inside of us for the world to see.

God loves you and has perfectly equipped you.

"Study to show yourself approved by God, a workman who need not be ashamed, rightly dividing the word of truth" (2 Timothy 2:15).

The lost need to know that they too have worth, but they cannot do it if we as Christians can't.

6. Are you ready to live out your eternal value and worth no matter who rejects you on earth?

If you have given the enemy a foothold because of what others have said or done to you, or you have diminished perception of your worth because of a sin you committed, it's time to repent, renew and refocus. God's plan for you and the value you are in his eyes are unchanging.

"For by grace you have been saved through faith, and this is not of yourselves. It is the gift of God, not of works, so that no one should boast. For we are His workmanship, created in Christ Jesus for good works, which God prepared beforehand, so that we should walk in them" (Ephesian 2:8-10).

Everything in this world, and everyone's opinion about yourselves, will one day all burn. All that will remain is Jesus. As believers, we need to live out the remainder of our days for the only things that matters, the value and worth of Jesus, which is eternal and immeasurable.

"For no one can lay another foundation than that which was laid, which is Jesus Christ. Now if anyone builds on this foundation with gold, silver, precious stones, wood, hay, or stubble, each one's work will be revealed. For the Day will declare it, because it will be revealed by fire, and the fire will test what sort of work each has done" (1 Cor. 3:11-13).

Remember who you are and who you belong to!

"But you are a chosen race, a royal priesthood, a holy nation, a people for God's own possession, so that you may declare the goodness of Him who has called you out of darkness into His marvelous light" (1 Pet. 2:8-9).

Please do not let one more second go by without accepting love that will never fail you!

If you have never accepted Jesus in your heart, it is time to meet your One and Only Love! Pray this prayer with me!

"Father God, I need Your love. I have been looking in all the wrong places, and I have had a revelation that You love me. Thank you for sending your Son Jesus to die for my sins and

heal my broken heart. Thank you for Your resurrection power, and that through Jesus, I am fully saved, forgiven and accepted. I confess my sins and ask you to forgive me. I want a fresh start. I need redirection. I want to be restored to be all You created me to be. I accept you Jesus as Lord and Savior and invite you into my heart. I will follow You on this new adventure, and I thank you for being the love of my life now and forever. In the precious name of Jesus, Amen."

Reflection Time

---

*Everything in this world,
and everyone's opinion
about yourselves, will
one day all burn. All that
will remain is Jesus.*

If you just received Jesus as your Lord and Savior, share your heart on your new love walk with Him, or if you rededicated your life to Jesus, how do you feel now?

_____

_____

_____

_____

_____

_____

_____

_____

_____

_____

_____

_____

_____

_____

_____

_____

_____

_____

_____

_____

_____

_____

_____

Chapter 8
Living Eternally Restored

Once we have experienced a revelation of God's eternal presence during seasons of earthly loneliness, desire Him above all else and intentionally redirect our thoughts to the beauty we can share being eternally connected to Jesus, we will start to experience restoration in each area of our lives. It doesn't all happen at once, and it may not come in the way we expect, but when we choose to see our earthly journey through the lens of heaven, we can experience eternal transformations that will bring peace, joy and the restoration our hearts long for.

As we face the trials of this life and the sting that comes from the pain we experience in our present lives, as we intentionally fix our eyes on Jesus and the eternity to come, we can trust and believe that 1) what we are facing on this earth is only for a season; 2) God is with us turning every hard time around for His good; 3) we can stay connected to him 24/7 through prayer, His Word and praying in the Holy Spirit and 4) we can live a life of abundance as our desires, goals and action align with God's perfect will and plan for our lives.

Here are nine passages to encourage and remind believers of the benefits of intentionally living singled out and set apart for God:

1. Determine in your heart that the trials you are facing right now are only for a season.

God shows us that on this earth everyone will experience ups and downs. We were not guaranteed that our earthly lives would be pain-free, because we live in an imperfect world. However, we must stay encouraged in the promise that this is only for a season:

"To everything there is a season, a time for every purpose under heaven: a time to be born, and a time to die; a time to plant, and a time to uproot what is planted; a time to kill, and a time to heal; a time to break down, and a time to build up; a time to weep, and a time to laugh; a time to mourn, and a time to dance; a time to cast away stones, and a time to gather stones; a time to embrace, and a time to refrain from embracing; a time to gain, and a time to lose; a time to keep, and a time to cast away; a time to tear, and a time to sew; a time to keep silence, and a time to speak; a time to love, and a time to hate; a time of war, and a time of peace". (Eccl.3:1-8)

2. Hold on to the eternal promises of God.

God knows the beginning from the end, and we do not. The longing we feel right now will not be satisfied with anything the world offers. The eternal hope God placed in our hearts is only found in Jesus.

"What benefit does the worker have in his toil? I have seen the task that God has given to sons of men to be concerned with. He has made everything beautiful in its appropriate time. He has also put obscurity (eternity) in their hearts so that no one comes to know the work that God has done from the beginning to the end. I experienced that there is nothing better for them than to be glad and do good in their life. And also, that everyone should eat and drink and experience good in all their labor. This is a gift of God. I have perceived that everything that God has done will be lasting. And to this there is nothing to be added, and from it there is nothing to be taken away". (Ecclesiastes 3:9-14)

3. Reflect on how Jesus stayed eternally connected to God.

Before Jesus left this earth, He was about to face the ultimate rejection from those He came to save. He was about to experience what we felt without the presence of God. However, He knew the pain he was about to experience was for a moment—a life-changing moment that would change history:

Do you now believe? Listen, the hour is coming. Yes, it has now come that you will be scattered, each to his own home, and will leave Me alone. Yet I am not alone, for the Father is with Me. I have told you these things so that in Me you may have peace. In the world you will have tribulation. But be of good cheer. I have overcome the world (John 16:31-33).

4. Know that you have an eternal Savior living inside you.

Jesus overcame so we could overcome. Without Him, all hope was lost. We may experience a "good and peaceful" life on this earth, but it will not make any difference because without Jesus, we are guaranteed an eternity in hell. However, through the sacrificial love of Jesus, we all can experience eternal life. "I have been crucified with Christ. It is no longer I who live, but Christ who lives in me. And the life I now live in the flesh, I live by faith in the Son of God, who loved me and gave Himself for me" (Gal. 2:20).

5. Remain in Jesus.

Knowing about eternal life through Jesus is a start in the right direction, but it isn't enough. Jesus told us we need to intentionally stay connected to His Holy Spirit to fulfill our eternal destinies:

Remain in Me, as I also remain in you. As the branch cannot bear fruit by itself, unless it remains in the vine, neither can you, unless you remain in Me. I am the vine, you are the branches. He who remains in Me, and I in him, bears much fruit. For without Me you can do nothing. As we remain in Him and He remains in us, we are empowered to do what He called us to do in this earth (John 15:4-5).

6. See past your earthly roles.

We may have many roles in our earthly lives. We may have the role of parent, pastor, caregiver, teacher, manager, spouse, leader, student and so on, but that is not who we are. We are the hands and feet of Jesus, who lives inside of us to reach a lost and dying world.

Every earthly role we play is temporary, but what we do as Christ's ambassadors last forever. "For I create new heavens and a new earth; the former things shall not be remembered or come to mind" (Isa. 65:17).

7. Align your earthly desires with God's eternal plan.

Our lives are not wasted and meaningless. Our lives aren't over because we didn't get everything we expected or wanted. At the end of this age, our lives are just about to begin. The eternal riches of God are worth more than we will ever gain on earth.

The Lord is the portion of my inheritance and of my cup; You support my lot. The lines have fallen for me in pleasant places; yes, an inheritance is beautiful for me. I will bless the Lord who has given me counsel; my affections also instruct me in the night seasons. I have set the Lord always before me; because He is at my right hand, I will not be moved. Therefore, my heart is glad, and my glory rejoices; my flesh also will rest in security. For You will not leave my soul in Sheol [pit, abyss, destruction], nor will You suffer Your godly one to see corruption.

You will make known to me the path of life; in Your presence is fullness of joy; at Your right hand there are pleasures for evermore (Ps. 16:5-11).

8. Believe that through Jesus, there is eternal transformation.

We must think about how much Jesus has done for us already and will continue to do if we trust Him in every season.

"We also were once foolish, disobedient, deceived, serving various desires and pleasures, living in evil and envy, filled with hatred and hating each other. But when the kindness and the love of God our Savior toward mankind appeared, not by works of righteousness which we have done, but according to His mercy He saved us, through the washing of rebirth and the renewal of the Holy Spirit, whom He poured out on us abundantly through Jesus Christ our Savior, so that, being justified by His grace, we might become heirs according to the hope of eternal life". (Titus 3:3-7)

9. Live eternally restored.

God promised that those who are in Christ will be made new. Receive it, believe it and live it!

"The Spirit Himself bears witness with our spirits that we are the children of God, and if children, then heirs: heirs of God and joint-heirs with Christ, if indeed we suffer with Him, that we may also be glorified with Him" (Rom. 8:16-17).

No matter who or what hurt us in this life, restoration begins when we see, believe and act upon the fact that God is preparing us for kingdom eternity and using us to bring others into that eternity. If we live our lives knowing this our only purpose for being here, and that our purpose is vital to the kingdom of God, we will see our lives in a whole new way.

Determine today that you will block out the voice of the enemy and the rejection from this world. Choose today to remain unshakeable in knowing your eternal value and worth!

If you have already accepted Jesus as Lord and Savior, are you ready to fall in love with Jesus all over again? Are you ready to open yourself to receive His love in full, heal you and bring the revelation, redirection and restoration needed to do what He has called you to do? We can stand together to encourage, speak truth and love one another in unity!

We do not have much time left. We are at the end of the age and you are so desperately needed by God to fulfill His great commission on this earth? Are you ready to come before the throne of God and fall in love? Pray this prayer with me!

"Father God, I am ready to fall in love again. This life has brought me pain and disappointment, but You are here to bring me hope, joy and restoration. Thank you for sending Jesus to make my life complete in You. I am sorry for trying to find love in my own strength and on my own terms. I commit my life to You fully. Give me a fresh revelation of your love on this new journey. I will follow Your direction. Redirect my priorities, hopes and dreams to align with Yours. I thank you that Your restoration over every area of my life will be greater than anything I could ever imagine! I

*receive Your love and love You! I pray these
things in the loving name of Jesus I pray, Amen!*

As we conclude this journey together,
remember, your story has just begun!

You have purpose and value. If life did not
originally turn out the way you thought, take
heart and be encouraged! As you fall in love
with Jesus again and again and allow God to
turn your life around the way He intended, get
ready for the adventure of your lifetime!

Reflection Time

No matter who or what hurt us in this life, restoration begins when we see, believe and act upon the fact that God is preparing us for kingdom eternity and using us to bring others into that eternity. If we live our lives knowing this our only purpose for being here, and that our purpose is vital to the kingdom of God, we will see our lives in a whole new way.

What will you do to live eternally restored?

_____

_____

_____

_____

_____

_____

_____

_____

_____

_____

_____

_____

_____

_____

_____

_____

_____

_____

_____

_____

_____

_____

_____

_____

Epilogue

When nobody could even possibly know what you are going through right now... Jesus does.

When nobody can see the cracks in your heart ready to give way...Jesus sees.

When you can't comprehend how many tears could possibly fall behind closed doors...Jesus understands.

When you feel the sting of rejection, betrayal and deception...Jesus feels.

When you fear there is no way out of your mess and brokenness...Jesus arrives.

When you cry out that you are ready to surrender it all...Jesus rescues.

When you admit that you tried to handle things your own way and fail...Jesus forgives.

When you let Him break down the walls you built to protect your shattered heart...Jesus heals.

When you realize He was there all of the time...Jesus reveals.

When you determine to change and live your life partner with His...Jesus redirects.

When you can share what He has done and is doing in your life, despite your circumstances, to a lost and dying world...Jesus restores.

About the Author

Dr. Meg Hart founded Restored Women in 2015. This ministry was birthed as a result of the great restoration she experienced through Jesus in her own life. She started the ministry to help women discover, embrace and live out their full God-given purposes, calls and destinies. She later added Restored Global to also to reflect her passion and vision to help bring God's restoration for everyone around the world.

She is an ordained pastor through Global Ministries and Relief, Inc. She holds a master's degree in Organizational Leadership from Regent University, and an EdD in Performance Improvement Leadership from Capella University.

She has written several articles for Charisma Magazine and serves as a leadership, public speaking and communications professor, trainer and consultant.

She is a proud mother of her daughter Mackenzie and serves at Life Church in Williamstown, NJ.

Contact Information

For more information on Dr. Meg Hart's Ministry, please visit:

Websites:
www.restoredglobal.com
www.drmeghart.com

Facebook:
http://facebook.com/restoredwomenglobal

Twitter:
@restored_women

Instagram:
@restoredglobal

Pinterest
https://www.pinterest.com/pastormeghart/

Email:
drmeghart@gmail.com

Made in the USA
Columbia, SC
20 June 2020

11657480R00067